Contents:

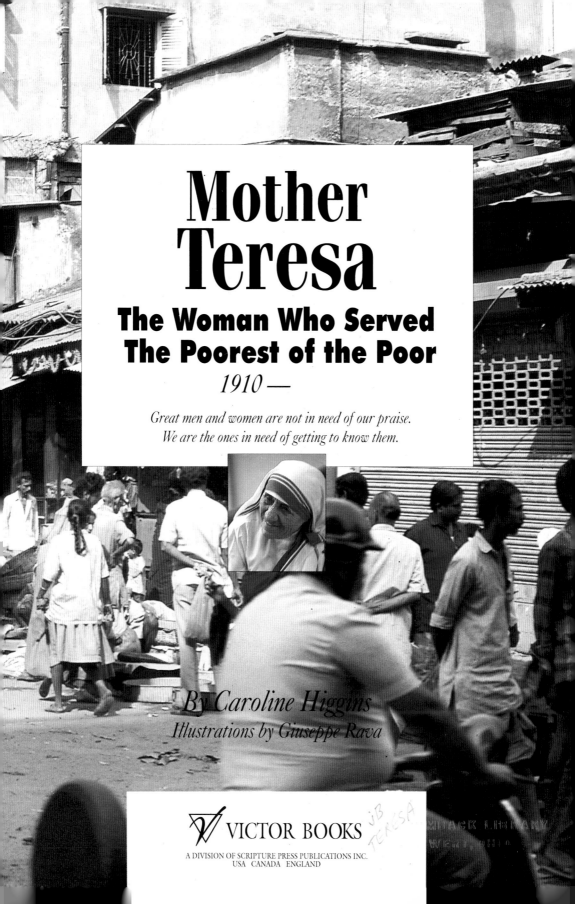

Mother Teresa

The Woman Who Served
The Poorest of the Poor

1910 —

Great men and women are not in need of our praise.
We are the ones in need of getting to know them.

By Caroline Higgins
Illustrations by Giuseppe Rava

VICTOR BOOKS

A DIVISION OF SCRIPTURE PRESS PUBLICATIONS INC.
USA CANADA ENGLAND

RATS, GARBAGE, AND A BOY WITH SAD EYES

Sister Teresa paused by the window of her simple bedroom on the second floor of the white marble building. At St. Mary's School and Convent in Calcutta, India she had a happy life teaching the children of wealthy British and Indian families. But this evening she looked longer than usual upon the alleyways below her in one of Calcutta's worst slums, the Entally district.

Teresa saw a scene which vividly contrasted with that of the elegantly landscaped gardens and pathways behind the high walls of St. Mary's. She saw narrow streets cluttered with every stall or business imaginable — textile factories, chemical manufacturers, and lean-to shacks set up to sell religious statues or cheap jewelry. And people were living in between the stalls, sleeping everywhere, in cardboard houses, doorways and on sidewalks, even on the concrete islands in the middle of the city streets. Teresa opened her window for some fresh air, but closed it again promptly; the smells of Calcutta's streets were sometimes unbearable to her. Rotting food and garbage lay heaped in the gutters, where rats scurried about. Smoke from small cooking fires mixed with exhaust from cars and buses. Cattle, considered holy by the Hindu religion, roamed through the streets freely. Their ribs stood out from under their hides. They, too, had a hard time finding food and shelter.

A beggar woman sat on the sidewalk. Her crippled feet were curled under her filthy sari, the common dress worn by Bengali women.

"One rupee, sahib," she begged of the people walking by her.

Other women and men lay in their own vomit or waste beside her. Teresa knew they could not pay for hospital

care or doctors; many had been abandoned by families who did not even have enough food. Motorbikes and rickshaw drivers simply   steered around the sick and dying.

Sister Teresa's heart was heavy with sadness. Ever since she had been a child, she had felt sorry for people who were struggling to find a meal every day, or who were lonely or hurting.

She asked herself, *How can I continue to live a comfortable life when there is so much suffering outside the convent walls? Perhaps I could avoid looking out the window.*

5

Teresa remembered the orphan child she had met on a winter trip into the city. A biting wind had blown against her sari as she hurried along the street. The sound of a hacking cough had caused her to look around. She had seen a small boy crouching in a doorway of a run-down warehouse, soulful and sad. And she had hesitated, then stopped.

"Are you sick?" she had asked.

The boy could not have been more than five years old. He nodded in reply to her question.

"Where are your parents?"

"Have none," he had replied, turning his head. A coughing fit had come from deep within his chest. Teresa guessed that he had pneumonia.

"I'll bring you some tea," Teresa had said as she vanished into the

crowd. She was back in a few minutes.

Temporary comfort was all she had been able to offer the boy. She could hardly bring people off the street into the quiet studious atmosphere of St. Mary's. *There are millions more just like that boy,* she thought. *What good can one person do in this sea of human misery?*

That night, when the moon was high in the sky, Teresa's eyes snapped open. In her dream she had seen the open wounds of dying people covered with maggots and she had heard the helpless cries of babies thrown onto garbage heaps as if they were nothing more than unwanted leftovers.

"I must do something," she determined the next morning.

CHILDHOOD GRIEF: A 10-YEAR-OLD LOSES HER FATHER

Teresa's childhood name was Agnes. She was 10 years old and living in Yugoslavia in the spring of 1920. Late one night, her sister Aga woke her up.

"Agnes! Agnes, come quickly," Aga said. "Father is ill, and the doctor is here."

Agnes shook her head, trying to focus on the meaning of her sister's words. She stumbled out of bed to join Aga, peering down the staircase into the room below.

"Nana, what's wrong with Papa?" Aga called down to her mother softly. Their brother Lazar appeared in a doorway. He was listening, too.

"Go back to bed, children, and say a prayer for Papa," their mother Drana responded. "We think it might be food poisoning."

Agnes thought soberly of Papa,

usually so busy in his construction business and in political activities, but never too busy to listen to her silly jokes and laugh with her. Agnes remembered the many times Papa had joined the children's games outdoors on hot summer evenings or had taken her swimming in the river. Eventually that night she fell asleep. But in the morning she woke to the sounds of sobbing.

"Father's dead, Agnes. Father died during the night," Aga wailed.

HER MOTHER TEACHES COMPASSION

The days passed slowly after her father's death, and there was a dull ache in Agnes' heart. Now the family business in the Yugoslavian town of Skopje was gone. Agnes' mother, Drana, was forced to support the family on her own. Drana started a small business in her home doing embroidery and handicrafts. She sold the second house the family had

always rented out. Eventually her business grew, and many women came to buy Drana's brightly colored towels, smocks, and wall hangings. Late one night there was a knock on the door. There stood a young woman, looking worried and in a hurry.

"Someone told me you do wonderful embroidery, but I've not come for that," she blurted out. "I'm very weak with a tumor, and my husband has left me. I was told I might find a place to stay here. I'm so sorry if I'm bothering you."

Drana's face softened with concern. She led the woman into the living room.

"Girls, put the kettle on and make up one of the beds, please," she told Aga and Agnes.

Agnes hesitated, knowing it was her bed that would go to their guest, while she would have to sleep with Aga. But she marched briskly into the kitchen where Aga was already setting the table for tea.

"Nana always says God calls us to serve Him and our neighbor," Agnes said to Aga. "Sometimes I don't like to hear it but I know she's right."

This was not the first time Drana had opened their home to the needy, but she always did it with little display. She often said, "Do good as if you were tossing a pebble into the sea." Agnes once helped her mother take a box of food to a poor family. She remembered many visits to a neighbor lady who was old and sick. Agnes noticed that helping people was a good way to get her mind off her own troubles and help her not feel so sad about her father's death.

Years later, Agnes said, "We were a very happy family. We lived for each

Teresa's Homeland

Teresa grew up in southeastern Europe, a part of the world that has been fought over for generations. When Teresa left home for India and until recently, it was known as Yugoslavia.

It is located on the Balkan peninsula just across the Adriatic Sea from Italy. This is a beautiful land with many mountains, lakes and sunny beaches. The Austrian composer Johann Strauss, Jr., was so inspired by the beauty of the Danube River

Yugoslavia at the time of Teresa's birth in 1910.

there that he wrote the famous "Blue Danube" waltz.

Sometimes earthquakes strike in the highland areas; in 1963 a major earthquake nearly leveled Skopje, Teresa's hometown and one of former Yugoslavia's largest cities.

This part of the world has been inhabited by many different kinds of people for hundreds of years. These groups moved into the area, bringing with them different languages and different ways of life.

The Croats called their region Croatia, and the Serbs established Serbia.

Other groups inhabiting the area include the Bosnians, Muslims, Macedonians, and Slovenes, as well as the Albanians and Turks. The country has three major religions, three official languages and two alphabets.

During Teresa's childhood all the different regions were united as one independent kingdom, eventually called Yugoslavia. After World War II it became a Communist state under the leadership of Josip Tito. In recent years, when other regions in that part of the world became independent of the USSR, Yugoslavia also broke its Communist ties. Since then, however, the Serbs and Croats have been fighting bitterly in a violent civil war over who should control the land.

other, and we made each other's lives very full and very happy. I have never forgotten my mother. . . ."

For as long as Agnes could remember, Nana had taken the children to the Church of the Sacred Heart every morning and ended the day with family prayers.

"Love God with all your heart," Nana always told Aga, Agnes, and Lazar.

Agnes loved all the Church activities — acting in the Christmas plays, singing in the choir, even singing solo sometimes or playing her accordion. She began to wonder what it would be like to make solemn vows and become a nun in the Church, totally devoted to God and His work.

SHE FINDS HER CALLING

One day Agnes skipped along the busy boulevard between church and her home. The late afternoon sun glinted and bounced off the leaves of the lacy maple trees lining the street. She felt light-hearted and excited as she hurried to share with Nana the missionary stories she had heard at the Society of Mary, a Church group for girls that met after school every week. There were always missionaries visiting from faraway places or talks about projects to help the needy at home. Last year the group had worked together, making quilts for poor families in the neighborhood.

Agnes burst through the open door and found her mother knitting in the living room.

"Nana, Society was so great today," she bubbled over with enthusiasm. "Brother Anthony from India shared about his work with the orphan children. He brought pictures and said the children love the missionaries! I just love to hear about all those places with mysterious sounding names."

"I'm glad you enjoy it so much," Drana said. "Here, would you hold my yarn while I wind it into a ball?"

Agnes continued, "I wonder how you find out what God wants you to do with your life. One time, Father Jambrekovich told me that when you give your life to God's service, He will fill your heart with a calling, sort of a knowing inside to do a certain kind of work."

"That's right, my love. Just keep seeking God," Drana said.

A TEENAGE GIRL LEAVES HOME

Agnes put thoughts of the future out of her mind for the next few years. But when she was almost eighteen, she spoke again with the missionaries from India. Her earlier fascination with India was still alive.

"Could I be a missionary?" Agnes asked the priest.

"Yes, and since you've been tutoring other students during your school days," Father Jambrekovich said, "you might be happy as a missionary teacher. You could apply to join the Loreto nuns, who teach the daughters of India's leaders."

Making the decision to become a nun, especially in a foreign country, was not easy. A nun gave her whole life over to God. Nuns promised never to seek after money for themselves, never to get married, and to always obey God. But Agnes had a peaceful feeling inside about becoming a nun and serving God in India. It was what she wanted to do. She also felt it was what God wanted her to do.

Agnes made plans to leave her home country of Yugoslavia and travel west across Europe to Ireland, the headquarters of the Loreto nuns. There, women came from all over the world to be trained as missionary teachers. In Ireland, she would learn English, the official language of India.

Agnes' brother, Lazar, had left home to join the military. When he heard her news, he wrote back, "Have you lost your senses, leaving home to go halfway around the world? How can you leave mother and Aga?"

"Lazar, you serve a king of two million subjects, but I serve the King of the whole world!" Agnes answered. "Which of us do you think is in the better place?"

In those days leaving to become a missionary meant that Agnes would probably never return to Skopje, and never see her family again. There would be no money to use for travel. It was a family sacrifice. But Drana spent a day in prayer, then asked Agnes only to "be sure of your decision and strive only for God."

IRELAND: A NEW LANGUAGE AND A NEW WAY OF LIFE

In Ireland Agnes became a postulant, someone learning about becoming a nun. The young women were given time to decide if they were sure this was what they truly wanted to do with their lives. Agnes had to wear a dark, heavy habit, or robe, made of linen. The food was different, the English language strange, and there was a whole new way of living. Postulants learned about "the silence," when no one was allowed to talk from bedtime until the morning. This was a way of preparing them for Mass and Communion the next day. Silence was also maintained in the dining room, and the Bible was read during all the meals.

Agnes spent six weeks in Ireland. Then she started the long journey by ship and train to India. There she would begin her work as a teacher.

INDIA: THE MISSION COUNTRY

The train chugged into Darjeeling spewing steam and smoke as if exhausted from its long uphill journey. Traveling through rugged river valleys and thick jungle growth, it finally reached this scenic spot in the shadow of the Himalayan mountains. Darjeeling was one of India's most beautiful resort cities, built at the foot of a rugged mountain.

Emerging from the train station, Agnes began the long climb up three flights of stairs built onto the side of the mountain. This was in the middle of the city. She reached the Loreto School perched at the top and looked down on the bustle of Darjeeling below. *What a fascinating city,* she thought, *so many different kinds of people — Indians, British, Tibetans, Mongolians. And the narrow streets are so crammed with colorful markets, bazaars, and food stalls.*

Agnes settled in happily at the convent in Darjeeling. Her English skills improved quickly and she also learned Bengali, the common language of India. She studied the Bible and taught history and geography to the girls at the Loreto School.

After three years there, Agnes made her first promises to God to remain poor, chaste, and obedient to Him.

"I'm so excited," she wrote to her mother, "today I get my ring and will choose my new name!"

The thin gold ring she placed on the third finger of her hand meant that she was now married — but not to any ordinary man. A nun promises that she will be married to Christ alone.

The privilege of being a nun meant that she could also choose a new name. "I'll choose Teresa, after St. Teresa of Lisieux, the little French nun who died so young but kept a wonderful diary," Teresa said. "She wrote about doing the smallest jobs as per-

fectly as you can because you love God. I want to be like that." So Agnes became Sister Teresa.

CALCUTTA: A NEW ADVENTURE

Soon afterwards, Sister Teresa was transferred to work in Calcutta, India, at St. Mary's School. She enjoyed the peaceful, serene life inside the walls of St. Mary's. Every day was the same. Every morning she got up early for prayers and Mass. She spent the day teaching the girls and, just as in her childhood home, she ended the day in prayer. Teresa was a popular teacher; the girls loved her, and she soon became the principal of St. Mary's.

But Teresa could still not forget the horror of the **bustees**, the slums which she saw right outside the gates of St. Mary's. She could not forget the view from her window. Sometimes she took several students with her and went into the streets, bringing medicine or bandages to the sick, lying in the gutters.

One spring day Mother Cenacle said something that surprised Teresa

and the girls at St. Mary's. "Perhaps we could help some of the street children by bringing them into the convent to care for and teach them."

Soon, about twenty children had been brought inside the school, but the idea simply did not work. Over several months' time, the children ran away one by one. Teresa realized that life inside the convent was simply too different for these children. They just could not adjust.

TERESA'S SECOND CALLING FROM GOD

The years went by and Teresa remained at St. Mary's. In September 1946, it was time for her yearly spiritual retreat to the mountains near Darjeeling. There she could be alone for prayer and meditation. How she looked forward to it!

Teresa climbed the steps near the rear of the train and found a worn seat by a window. The train rolled slowly through the streets of Moti Jheel, the worst slum in Calcutta. It would eventually head out into the countryside on its way towards the mountains. Hissing and belching, the train stopped every few minutes at stations throughout the city, taking on more passengers.

Beggars, the hungry, and the homeless, were camped out on station platforms. With outstretched arms they asked the train's passengers for coins to be tossed their way. Trash lay everywhere. Traffic in the nearby streets swerved to avoid the potholes. Ragged, barefoot children wandered idly or sat playing games with stones from the gutter.

Teresa did not turn away from the scene outside the train window. Instead, the thought came back, *I must do something.*

"Lord, is that You speaking to me?" Teresa prayed.

Teresa thought of the Bible verse she had read so many times. *"I was hungry and you gave me no food; I was thirsty and you gave me no drink; I was a stranger and you took me not in,* *naked and you did not clothe me, sick and in prison and you did not visit me."* She remembered that Jesus had said if you helped the least important kind of people, it was the same as helping Him.

Teresa believed she was hearing the "still, small voice" of God speaking to her. She called this her "call within a call" to follow the Lord, not only to India, but now also into the slums. God was calling her to leave the convent and serve Him by living as a poor person and caring for the poorest of the poor. During her retreat time she prayed again and again about this.

OBSTACLES IN HER WAY

Teresa's hopes were high as she climbed the spacious staircase to the office of the Archbishop of Calcutta, the Church official who could give her permission to leave the Sisters of Loreto.

"I cannot give permission for one lone woman to go live on the streets. Wait a year and pray about it," he said.

The year passed slowly. On her second visit to the archbishop, he asked her to write the Mother General of the Loreto Nuns and Pope Pius XII for permission.

Mother Gertrude, the Mother General, wrote back, "If God is calling you, I give you permission with all my heart."

Teresa wrote to Pope Pius XII, requesting "to live alone outside the cloister among the poor of Calcutta, with God alone as protector and guide."

Not long afterwards, Teresa received the Pope's permission. But again, making a change was difficult.

"Leaving Loreto was much more difficult than leaving my family and country to enter religious life," Teresa said later. "Loreto, my spiritual training, my work, it meant everything to me."

But God was calling Teresa, and she followed Him.

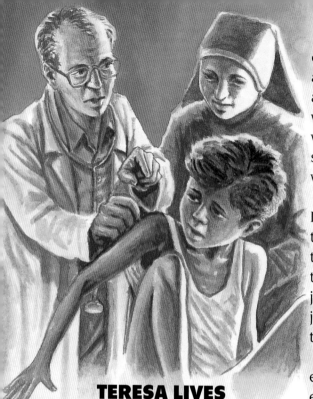

TERESA LIVES AS A POOR PERSON

Amidst tearful goodbyes, Teresa walked down the steps of St. Mary's and towards the train station. This train would not take her to the slums of Moti Jheel, but instead, to Patna, a city 240 miles away, where she would live and work with the Medical Mission Sisters for a time. Teresa knew she needed more medical training in order to help the sick people in the slums. She would spend the next four months learning how to give shots, administer medicine, first aid, and even how to deliver babies. She would learn to help patients suffering from the worst diseases — cholera, leprosy, smallpox.

One morning, Teresa stood talking with the sisters in the courtyard at the Medical Mission Hospital. On this particular day she was wearing something different. She had on a white cotton sari with three stripes of blue along the hem. It draped neatly across her tiny five-foot frame. This was the everyday dress worn by the women of India. She had pinned a small cross to her left shoulder and wore sandals on her feet.

"I'm not wearing my black veil and Loreto habit anymore," Teresa told the sisters. "I don't want to stand out too much. It's important for me and the sisters serving with me to dress just like the poor. We will eat only rice just as they do. We will preach Christ to them by the way we live."

But Mother Dengel of Patna objected to the food Teresa proposed to eat. "If you make your sisters eat only rice, you will commit a serious sin," she said. "How do you expect your sisters to work, if their bodies receive no sustenance? The very poor work very little, become sick and die young. But you must feed your sisters well. To resist disease, they must eat healthy food."

Teresa decided Mother Dengel was right. Her sisters would eat well.

India's Political History

eople often wonder, why is English spoken in India? Why did the British have so much influence in India?

Centuries ago, when European explorers like Christopher Columbus and Vasco da Gama found new trade routes to the Far East, the British East India Company established trad-

ing posts at Indian ports. During the 1700s when the Mogul Empire in India was dissolving, the British East India Company took over the country, attaining political power in 1757. A century later, the British government itself gained control, and in 1877 Queen Victoria became not only queen of England but empress of India.

As the twentieth century

began, there was much unhappiness among the Hindus and Muslims in India because of British rule. In 1919, after World War I ended, British troups fired on a crowd of Indian protestors, killing nearly 400 people and creating a climate of almost constant friction between the British and Indians.

When Sister Teresa first arrived in Calcutta, the Indian

INTO THE STREETS: ONE CHILD AT A TIME

Moti Jheel looked the same on this day in December, 1948 as any other day. The flies buzzed furiously on the heaps of human waste lying in dark corners; there were no sewers in many parts of Calcutta. Women sat on the sidewalks in front of their makeshift shelters, rocking wailing babies. Their faces looked worn and tired and thin. Sick men held up their hands pleading, as Teresa walked by. Teresa had five **rupees** — less than one dollar — in her pocket as she left Patna. Early this day, her first living in Calcutta's worst slum, she had already given away four rupees to the poor.

A priest approached her and asked if she had a few rupees she could give him for a Church newspaper. Teresa hesitated but gave the priest the one remaining rupee in her pocket.

How will I pay my rent? *How will I buy my own food, let alone help the poor?* These thoughts tumbled about in

independence movement was growing under the leadership of Mahatma Gandhi, an Indian lawyer who had been educated in London. In 1920 he became the leader of the Indian National Congress, India's most important political organization. Gandhi, a Hindu, believed strongly in living a simple life and in practicing tolerance for other people with different viewpoints. He believed in peacefully disobeying British laws if he felt they were unfair. Leading marches, sit-ins in the streets, and hunger strikes, he protested the British tax on salt and campaigned against a British law that would have made it illegal to organize opposition against the government. Many times Gandhi was jailed for his nonviolent disobedience; he felt it was honorable to be imprisoned for a worthy cause. Gandhi fasted many times to emphasize the importance of resolving issues peacefully. In time, more and more people joined Gandhi in supporting Indian independence.

During World War II the Japanese invaded neighboring Burma, and many Burmese refugees crossed into India. Sometimes there were Japanese bombing raids. Once, the sisters at Loreto had to evacuate their students to the countryside. In 1946 Muslims and Hindus clashed in bloody riots in Calcutta, killing 4,000 people. Sister Teresa went for food during the riot time and was stunned of the sight of so many dead

Teresa's mind, but her faith held steady. *No, she thought, if God is calling me, He will bless my work and never abandon me.*

But Teresa soon became exhausted. All day she had searched for a shelter for herself and a place where she could bring the abandoned. She walked until she could walk no more. She spent the day knocking on countless doors in the wealthier sections of Calcutta, asking for food to be donated to the poor. She asked for medical supplies and treated those in need as she met them. At some point she had stopped to hold a dying woman and comfort her. By the end of the day Teresa's arms and legs ached.

She wrote in her diary: "I couldn't feel sorry for myself because I thought how much the poor themselves must ache in body and soul, looking every day for a home and food and even good health."

Then, late that same day, the priest Teresa had seen earlier handed her

bodies in the streets.

Even though the British had granted additional rights to the Indian people in many areas, Indians still wanted to rule themselves. In 1947 the British gave independence to India. But the violence between Muslims and Hindus continued, so Indian and British leaders agreed that India should be divided into two parts. India would become a Hindu country, and a new country, Pakistan, would be created for the Muslims. Each would be an independent nation. Gandhi was very grieved by this separation of the two peoples as he had fought so hard for unity. He was assassinated in 1948 by a man who did not agree with his views.

Jawaharlal Nehru, who had worked with Gandhi for an independent India, became prime minister of the new nation. Its form of government was a democratic republic. In the years since, the Indian standard of living has improved and industry expanded, but continuing rivalries among ethnic groups and border disputes still cause considerable strife. In the past ten years there have been two assasinations of Indian prime ministers. Indira Gandhi, who was Nehru's daughter and no relation to Mahatma Gandhi, was assasinated in 1984, and her son Rajiv Gandhi was assasinated in 1991. Today P.V. Narasimha RAO is prime minister and S. D. Sharma is India's president.

an envelope containing fifty rupees. It was a gift from a man who had heard about Teresa's work and wanted to help. She had learned her first lesson about trusting God fully.

And yet the job before her seemed impossible. *Where do I begin?* she thought. *Where do I start? There are so many needs everywhere. Out of love for God, I desire to remain.* "Give me courage," she prayed.

The sight of so many wandering, ragged children tore at Teresa's heart. She would begin with the children. She cleared a spot in the street and began writing letters from the Bengali alphabet in the dirt with a stick. Some children gathered around her. Then she talked with them about what the letters meant. They were

intrigued, as if it were some sort of secret code. A few days later there were thirty children coming to Teresa's school of the streets.

Teresa brought soap and water, and the children took turns getting washed. What a new experience this was for most of them! But it felt good and fresh. She gave out bars of soap for coming to school every day. Teresa brought them milk at noontime.

In the evenings Teresa cared for the sick and dying. Sometimes she felt overwhelmed by the screams of the sick, the smell of gangrene and vomit, and the long hours of backbreaking work. She remembered the peace and cleanliness of St. Mary's and was tempted to quit. But Teresa, called of God, was not a quitter.

When asked how she did manage to keep going, Teresa said, "One child at a time, one child at a time. If I can only help the closest one, that will be enough. And I feel it is the Lord I tend in the poor. It is His wounds I bathe, His sores I clean, His wounds I bandage."

Some of the sisters from St. Mary's came to the streets of Moti Jheel to see what Teresa was doing. They brought supplies she could use in her outdoor school. A priest helped her find a permanent place to live upstairs in a certain house. She was allowed to live there for free by the owner, Michael Gomes, an Indian teacher. He even provided her with food.

A REVOLUTION OF LOVE: TERESA'S HELPERS

One evening a knock at the door pulled Teresa away from her prayers. There stood Shubashini Das, one of Teresa's former students, a petite Bengali girl, smaller even than Teresa.

"Sister, I have come to join you," Shubashini said. "I know it will be a hard life but I am prepared for it."

"Come in, come in," Teresa replied, "Let's talk."

"You need to realize," Teresa said, "there will be only just enough to eat . . . the expensive saris will be replaced with the white cotton ones. . . we will not have fans in our rooms in the sweltering heat because the poor do not have fans . . . we will be caring for and loving society's outcasts. And all this must be entered into with a joyful heart."

"I'm ready, Sister," said Shubashini softly.

Soon more of Teresa's former students arrived. Shubashini became Sister Agnes. Sister Gertrude, Sister Margaret, Sister Bernard and others moved one by one into the upper story of Michael Gomes' house.

It was the beginning of the order of sisters Teresa had hoped for. She called them the Missionaries of Charity. The sisters now called her Mother Teresa. All nuns take the three vows of poverty, chastity, and obedience. But the Missionaries of Charity would have a fourth: to serve the poorest of the poor.

Teresa was excited. She wrote to her mother Drana, "It is beautiful to see our young people fully devoted, full of love for God's poor! What a wonderful gift of God. It is not the excitement of the work that is drawing them. It is something much deeper and more wonderful . . . it is a living miracle that impresses hundreds of people, even non-Christians, who come close to the sisters."

The sisters woke up every morning at 4:30 for prayers and Communion. "We must get the love and strength we need for the day from the Lord," Teresa said. "We are not social workers; we are in the business of doing something beautiful for God."

Then, after breakfast, the sisters washed one of their two white saris in a tin bucket, hung it out to dry, and mopped the floor by hand. Again Teresa insisted, "We will not have any modern conveniences that the poor do not have; we will do everything just as they do."

Eventually there were more than ten sisters living in Michael Gomes' upper floor, all sleeping side by side.

Teresa began praying for a larger place to live. Soon she heard of a Muslim man who wanted to give his house to the sisters.

"I received this house from God. Now I give it back to Him," he said.

The Missionaries of Charity moved into the first house of their own at 54a Lower Circular Road, Calcutta.

The house was a quiet, peaceful haven where the sisters could become rested and refreshed before going back out to serve the suffering. Others like it would eventually be given to the sisters all over the world.

A PLACE TO LOVE THE DYING

The early morning sun sparkled and danced on the tin roof of the shanty. A garbage truck was parked in front of it. Teresa watched the dark-skinned men lift a dead body into the truck. This was something she had often seen, bodies being collected that had died on the street during the night.

She spoke to Sister Margaret, who stood next to her. "The biggest disease today is not leprosy or cancer or tuberculosis, but rather the feeling of being unwanted, uncared for, deserted by everybody."

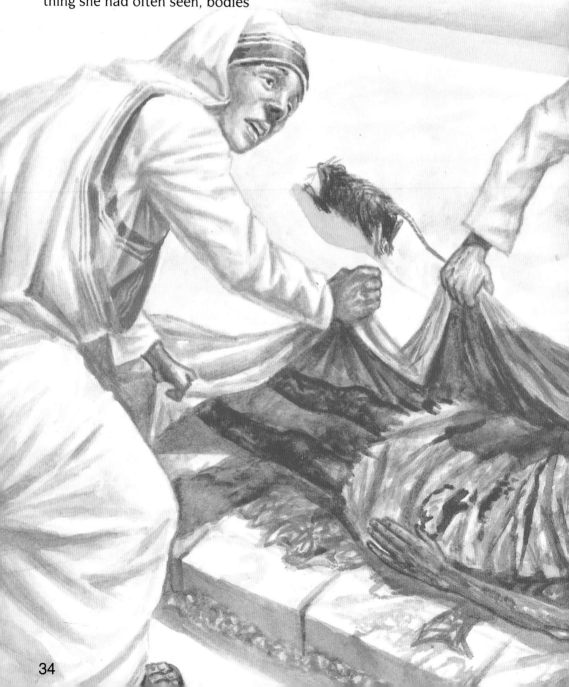

The two sisters walked on and turned the next corner. There something caught Teresa's eye. Near a trash bin she saw a heap of rags covering a body. *Another one to be picked up,* she thought. As she pulled the tattered cloth away from the body, Teresa gasped. Three rats scurried off it as she saw a woman's body, the feet eaten away by rats. Ants writhed on the open sores. The woman stirred slightly. She was not yet dead!

"She was dropped off to die here, no doubt," said Teresa. "People take better care of their dogs and cats, than they do their fellow human beings!"

Mother Teresa and Sister Margaret half dragged the woman to a nearby hospital. But the hospital refused to admit her. "She is too far gone for us to try and save her," was their reply. Teresa's strong will held firm.

"I will stay here until you admit her," she said with determination. The hospital gave in and admitted the dying woman.

People in India didn't help others very readily. Many were Hindus who believed that if a person was suffering, that was just his **karma**, or the hardship he had to endure because of what he had done in a past life. No one was supposed to help him.

The experience with the dying woman made Teresa more desperate than ever to find a place where she could bring such people. She wanted somewhere where they could die sur-rounded by love and kindness. She went to the city officials. They suggested the back rooms of Kalighat, a Hindu temple. There, three rooms, unused for months — and filthy — were promptly cleaned by the sisters.

A week later the first patients were moved into what Teresa called Nirmal Hriday, "the place of the pure heart." The sisters went out daily and brought in from the streets the dying of every race and every religion. Teresa washed and comforted the Hindu priest dying of cholera even though it meant she was in danger of catching the disease herself. Sister Frederick spoke words of love as she picked maggots off the wounds of a Muslim woman. The sisters respected each person's religious beliefs and did not try to change them.

India's Caste System

Untouchables! Those people are untouchables!" These words tell a story of India's social system, which had been in existence for thousands of years. It was finally outlawed in this century, just about the time Mother Teresa was working in India.

People in India used to be divided into groups, called the caste system.

If a person was born into one class, or caste, he couldn't change to another. He or she couldn't marry someone in a different caste. Sometimes it was even against the law for people to speak to someone from another caste.

The priests and scholars were on the highest rung of the caste system "ladder." They were called the Brahmans. Next came the rulers and soldiers, called Kshatriyas. The artists and merchants were the Vaisyas. Servants and laborers were called the Sudras. And at the lowest level were people who did not belong to any

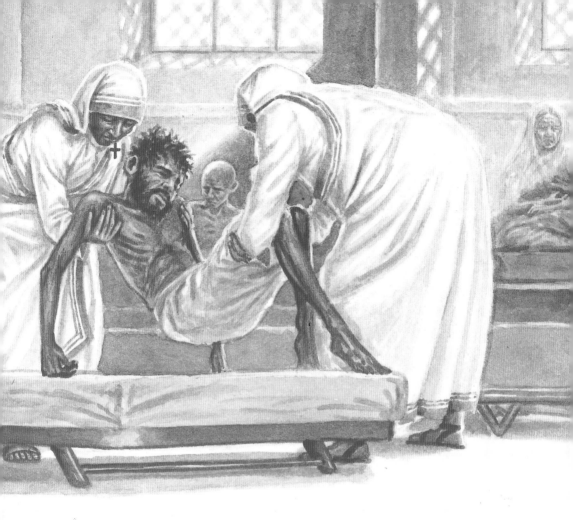

other groups so they were called the pariahs, or untouchables.

The Hindu religion teaches said that people are reincarnated, that is they come back after death in another body. The only way a person could move to another caste was by living righteously and following the Hindu law in this life. Then there would be hope of being born into another caste in the next life.

Mother Teresa battled this ancient form of prejudice when she reached out to help the poorest of the poor, India's "untouchables." It was not a popular thing to do. Many in India thought the poor people were suffering because of their behavior in previous lives and that they deserved it.

Due to Mother Teresa's example, many families spoke out against this prevailing social philosophy. Some from highclass families came to Shishu Bhavan to adopt the orphans there.

A well-known Indian leader, Mahatma Ghandi, was also battling the caste system about the same time. He taught that people should accept all different kinds of people and their creeds and religions. He was assassinated in 1948 by a high-ranking Brahman who feared these ideas.

A few years later, in 1955, India's caste system was outlawed.

But many of the neighbors complained, "Why are they bringing these stinking people into our neighborhood? Are they trying to convert them to Christianity?"

Once, a group of men surrounded Mother Teresa and threatened to kill her. "You will just simply send me to Heaven sooner then," she had said. They turned and walked out the door.

Local Hindus were upset and accused Teresa of all sorts of crimes. They sent the chief of police to assess the situation. As he walked through the rooms, the man saw sister after sister washing away the filth, giving painkillers, and speaking words of comfort to the destitute people.

Stepping outside the building to address the angry Hindus, the police chief said, "Unless you can get your own mothers and sisters to come

here and care for these dying people, I will not make the Missionaries of Charity leave." The angry Hindus turned and walked away.

Once, an atheist came to the Home for the Dying. He watched a sister care for a man covered with maggots. He said to Mother Teresa, "I came here godless. I came here full of hatred. I am going full of God. I have seen God's love in action. Now I believe."

Suddenly public opinion started to change. People from the community stopped complaining and started volunteering to help. Medical companies donated supplies. Some people offered to pray regularly. One woman, Ann Blaikie, organized her friends to provide clothing. They became known as the Co-Workers of Mother Teresa. Today there are groups of Co-Workers all over the world.

GARBAGE-HEAP BABIES

One afternoon, Sister Marguerite and Sister Agnes were walking through Moti Jheel. Alert to the sights and sounds of the slum, they were searching for anyone who might need help. They fingered their rosary beads, praying as they went. The noisy din of the street was all around them — cattle bawling, the cries of vendors selling their wares, beggars calling out, the roar of cars and motorbikes. Then they heard the insistent, helpless cries of a newborn baby and followed the sound. A baby, not much larger than a man's hand, lay naked on a heap of cow dung near a pile of garbage. Sister Marguerite picked up the child, swaddled it in her sari, and the two nuns carried the baby four streets further, to Shishu Bhavan, a decaying gray building with a cross

on the side.

This place was Mother Teresa's newest project. There were so many orphans. There were many children starving to death. There were many children who had simply been abandoned. Teresa had dreamed of a place for such children, and in 1955 Shishu Bhavan became a reality.

One night Mother Teresa heard a child crying at the gates of Shishu Bhavan. She found a small boy, not more than six years of age. Tears were running down his cheeks.

"I went to my father and my father didn't want me," he sobbed. "I went to my mother and my mother didn't want me. Do you want me?"

Yes, they did.

Dark-haired Rani, a mother at sixteen, sat in one corner of the big room and cradled another small boy in her arms. She could not support her son and had nowhere to turn but Shishu Bhavan. The boy's legs were grotesquely deformed. Mother Teresa

reached out and stroked the boy's head. "So beautiful," she whispered, smiling.

At Shishu Bhavan children of all ages were loved and fed, educated and made well. Sometimes the oldest child in a poor family from the streets was sent to public school by the sisters, so that he might help the others. Sometimes the sisters found husbands for the older girls. In Indian culture it is very important for a girl to find a husband and to have a dowry, gifts or money, to give him when they marry. Also, Teresa found parents to adopt children, even in faraway lands. People from India also came to adopt children from the Missionaries of Charity.

More and more people began to hear of Mother Teresa and her work. They sent money to her so she could support the children. Shishu Bhavan began to meet more needs. It became a clinic, a shelter for young unmarried, expectant mothers, and a soup kitchen.

"TOUCH A LEPER: TOUCH HIM WITH LOVE"

The ragged man looked grotesque. He sat in a dark doorway at the back of a warehouse. People who happened to look at him quickly turned their eyes away. He had no fingers, no toes, no ears; he did not even have a nose. There were just lumps of hardened flesh where these had been. He rarely came out into the daylight.

The man had a hideous disease that scared people more than any other — no one wanted to come near a person with leprosy. Leprosy is an ancient disease, dating back to biblical times. In those days a leper was required to ring a bell and call out, "Unclean, unclean" so that people would stay away. Leprosy spreads mainly where people are living closely together in unhealthy situations. Teresa knew there were many people with leprosy in Calcutta. She had seen them trying to hide themselves away, unable to work, abandoned by their families, digging through garbage for food.

"I must do something," she said again.

Mother Teresa went to the city officials. She knew that leprosy could now be treated and lepers could be healed if the disease was caught soon enough.

"Are there any hospitals in Calcutta that treat leprosy?" she asked. But the answer that came back to her was "No."

The place where Calcutta's many thousands of leprous people lived spread out along the railroad tracks. Teresa knew there were thousands of lepers in Calcutta, and maybe as many as fifty thousand in all of India. Inside one of the thrown-together shacks, one leper was bandaging another. They helped each other. There was no one else who was willing to do so. The woman dragged herself across the room; her foot was gone. She had lost all feeling in her deformed hands. There was no running water, no toilet facilities.

Teresa found a doctor, Dr. Senn, who, touched by the work of the Missionaries of Charity, left his own practice. He joined the sisters in their

efforts to help the lepers. He began training the nuns to care for them.

Mother Teresa said, "When we ask our young sisters who would like to go and work with the lepers, every hand is up. Every sister sees Christ in the lepers, even though they are disfigured."

The Missionaries of Charity decided they needed mobile vans equipped with medical supplies that could travel all over the city to treat the lepers in their own communities. To raise money for the vans, the sisters used the slogan, "Touch a Leper: Touch Him With Love." Money poured in from all over India.

But this wasn't enough for Mother Teresa. She wanted the lepers to have a beautiful place to live, and not be pushed away, living on borrowed property. She wanted them to be able to learn skills, grow gardens, support themselves without begging, and feel pride in themselves. She even wanted them to be able to die in a place surrounded by love and peace. Eventually, in 1957, Shantinagar, the Place of Peace, was built on donated land. It consisted of several small houses with trees and gardens.

At a Christmas party at Shantinagar, Mother Teresa told the lepers, "You are a gift from God. God has a special love for you."

An old man, deformed and misshapen, crawled up to Teresa. "I have always heard nobody loves me. It's wonderful to know that God loves me. Please say that again!"

MOTHER TO THE WHOLE WORLD

"Still working? Yes, I'm still working," Mother Teresa told a newspaper reporter who had come to interview her. Her weathered brown face was smiling as she bent over a sick woman, changing a bandage. "Yes, I've been in India for almost thirty years. The hot Indian sun is wrinkling my face, my back is stooped from bending towards the needy, but I never intend to retire."

The year was 1966. Politics or social work did not interest Mother Teresa — only seeing Jesus in one more needy person, one at a time.

Her name began to be spoken around the world. Young women came knocking, wanting to join the Missionaries of Charity. The sisters, new and old, continued to live just like the poor, squeezed together in their big house. They had to be physically, spiritually, and emotionally healthy in order to handle the long hours of hard, sorrowful work. Just as important, they had to be cheerful and full of joy. Teresa said, "A smile is the beginning of love."

Advice from Mother Teresa

T each your family to be aware of the poor. Encourage them to go and do something for so many who are in need, for so many who are starving. Live simply. Give example through simplicity. The spirit of poverty is dependency on God. Trust him. Be with and love the poorest of the poor. You can and must expect suffering. It is a sign that Jesus is near when you are suffering. Jesus is very near, watching you.

Prayer is simply talking to God. He speaks to us: we listen. We speak to him: he listens. A two-way process: speaking and listening. Say this prayer often: "Jesus, in my heart, I believe in your tender love for me. I love you." The more you pray, the easier it becomes. The easier it becomes, the more you pray.

–from Mother Teresa, My Life for the Poor, Harper & Row, San Francisco 1985.

Even young men wanted to serve with Mother Teresa. So the Missionary Brothers of Charity was established. The brothers worked with the men and boys living on the streets and helped in places the sisters could not. Other people came to volunteer for short periods of time.

A British television producer, Malcolm Muggeridge heard about Mother Teresa and came to do a documentary about her in 1969. He called it **Something Beautiful for God.** In the film, Teresa did not ask for money for her order or help for

her sisters; she simply told people to love and understand their own neighbors and families.

Years passed. At Shishu Bhavan seven thousand people were being fed every day. People asked Mother Teresa to start Missionary houses in Rome and Bombay and New York and Caracas. The blue-striped saris of the sisters began to be seen all around the world.

To Mother Teresa nothing was impossible. "If God is doing it," she said, "He will bless it. We do nothing. He does everything. God has not called me to be successful. He called me to be faithful."

Sometimes Teresa needed to board a plane to travel to the Missionary houses in faroff places, but she had no money of her own. She asked one airline if she could pay her way by working as a stewardess! The prime minister of India, Indira Gandhi, heard about it and was amazed. She promptly arranged for Teresa to have a free pass on Air India flights anytime she wanted! Sometimes Teresa saved the food she received on the flights for the poor.

When the Pope visited India, he gave Mother Teresa the white Lincoln Continental limousine that had been given to him. Yet Mother Teresa had no use for such a luxury car. She promptly raffled it off for many rupees and used the money to help her lepers.

Awards and prizes of every description began to pour in for Mother Teresa's work. She received many honorary degrees, an award for International Understanding and the Peace Prize from Pope John XXIII. She was often invited to speak. Although she didn't enjoy it, she went anyway. It was an opportunity to tell people that we must all become carriers of God's love.

One day, one of the world's greatest honors came her way. Mother Teresa, almost seventy years old, was to be awarded the Nobel Peace Prize. She went to Oslo, Norway in 1979 to accept the award. On her way to speak before kings and presidents, she said, "I am unworthy."

Mother Teresa's message was simple: "You have an opportunity to love others as God loves you — in the

The Nobel Peace Prize

Alfred Nobel became one of the world's richest men in 1867 when he invented dynamite. His father was an inventor, and he was a chemist in Sweden. But over the years Nobel began to regret that he had created a substance which caused death and injury, and he feared it might be used for war. So he used some of his money to reward people for furthering the cause of peace in the world.

He set up the Nobel Prizes. They are awarded every year in six different areas to people who have done or created something for the good of all people everywhere. Awards are given in the fields of science, economics, medicine and literature.

Mother Teresa won the award for outstanding work in the interest of international peace. The awards consist of a medal and cash, usually over $150,000. A committee of five people, elected by the Norwegian parliament, chooses the winner of the peace prize. Winners receive their awards every year in Oslo, Norway. The prize is awarded on December 10th, the anniversary of the death of Alfred Nobel.

small things, with great love." She asked that the awards banquet be cancelled; the poor were the ones who needed the food.

Teresa decided not to accept any more awards; they took too much time away from her work with the poor. Even into her eighties, Teresa is visiting her houses, helping, speaking, praying. She calls herself a "little pencil in the hand of God." He does the thinking and the writing, she tells people, the pencil has only to be allowed to be used.

Main Events in Mother Teresa's Life

1910 Agnes Bojaxhiu is born on August 27th in Skopje, Macedonia.

1929 Agnes arrives in Darjeeling, India to work as a novice nun at the Loreto School and takes the name Teresa.

1931 Sister Teresa moves to Calcutta and begins teaching at St. Mary's School.

1937 Sister Teresa takes her final vows of service to the Church.

1946 On the train to Darjeeling, Sister Teresa receives "a call within a call" to serve the poorest of the poor.

1948 Sister Teresa leaves the convent and begins her work in the slums.

1950 Mother Teresa founds and heads the Missionaries of Charity.

1952 Mother Teresa opens Kalighat, a home for the dying in Calcutta.

1955 Mother Teresa opens Shishu Bhavan, the first children's home, in Calcutta.

1959 Mother Teresa opens the first leprosy clinic.

1965 Houses for Missionaries of Charity are opened outside India.

1979 Mother Teresa receives the Nobel Peace Prize in Oslo, Norway.

1981 Mother Teresa celebrates fifty years of service to God and people as a nun.

1983 Mother Teresa is admitted to the hospital for heart disease but recovers.

1983 The Missionaries of Charity help those injured by the poisonous gas leaked by a pesticide plant in Bhopal, India.

1994 The Missionaries of Charity have 3,439 sisters in 537 houses in 114 countries worldwide.

1994 Mother Teresa speaks in Washington, D.C. at the United States National Prayer Breakfast attended by President Clinton.

BOOK RESOURCES

Egan, Eileen, Such a Vision of the Street, Doubleday & Company, Inc., Garden City, New York, 1985.

Giff, Patricia Reilly, Mother Teresa: Sister to the Poor, Viking Kestrel, Penguin Books, USA, Inc., New York, New York, 1986.

Gray, Charlotte, Mother Teresa, Gareth Stevens Publishing, Milwaukee, Wisconsin, 1988.

Jacobs, William Jay, Mother Teresa, The Millbrook Press, Brookfield, Connecticut, 1991.

Johnson, Linda Carlson, Mother Teresa, The Rosen Publishing Group, Inc., New York, New York, 1991.

Mother Teresa, Contemplative in the Heart of the World, Servant Books, Ann Arbor, Michigan, 1985.

Mother Teresa, My Life for the Poor, Harper and Row Publishers, San Francisco, California, 1985.

Serrou, Robert, Teresa of Calcutta, McGraw-Hill Book Company, Maidenhead, England, 1980.

Watson, D. Jeanene, Teresa of Calcutta, Mott Media, Milford, Michigan, 1984.

MISSIONARIES OF CHARITY AROUND THE WORLD

LET US DO SOMETHING BEAUTIFUL FOR GOD

From Calcutta to Delhi to Bombay, the Missionaries of Charity began by carrying on their work throughout India. Within a few years, they were serving all over the world. Today there are over 3,000 sisters and 537 houses serving the poor in 114 countries. Forty-two new houses opened in 1994 alone, including those in Stockholm and Tunisia. People from all walks of life and of all nationalities have become co-workers either by contributing financial support, prayer, or volunteer work. They may be working alongside the sisters, or they may be serving the poor in their own cities. When a disabled woman asked how she could help, Mother Teresa suggested she organize a prayer group. This group now calls itself, "The Sick and Suffering," and they pray regularly for the work. Monasteries around the world pray for the sisters as well. For more information, please write to: **The Missionaries of Charity, 54A Lower Circular Road, Calcutta, 70016, India.**